Mastering The Mental Side
Of Winning

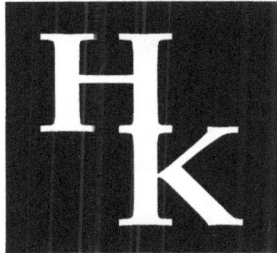

Hemispheric
Kinesiology

Ernest Solivan

Mastering The Mental Side Of Winning

ISBN: 978-0-578-03607-6

"If winning isn't everything why do they keep score."
Vince Lombardi

Table Of Contents

Table Of Contents

Introduction

With the advent of quantum physics, science must now acknowledge that there are things that happen below our level of conscious awareness that dramatically affect the experiences we create. *Mastering The Mental Side Of Winning* is a book that explains a program designed to work on a quantum level, or below your level of conscious awareness. And, that is where the blockages are located preventing you from winning with more consistency using Hemispheric Kinesiology (HK).

HK is a muscle testing success technology that helps access, isolate and neutralize psychological blockages preventing you from successfully accomplishing your goals. It provides you with a perspective that allows you to objectively look at the experiences you are creating in your life and through that objectivity create positive change that will improve the quality of your life, and isn't that what we are all looking for?

HK's most salient characteristic is that it offers a very credible, rational and viable explanation as to why you experience performance problems during competition and provides a remedy that will allow you to enhance your ability to win no matter what the sport.

There is an old saying that you cannot teach an old dog new tricks. This is a testament to how difficult change is for just about everyone. There are basically three elements necessary to create change in your life.

They are Sensation, Perception and Conception. Sensation is the capacity to experience; Perception is the capacity to be aware of what you are experiencing; and Conception is taking action to begin the process of change, or it can also represent a rebirthing into some new experience.

I refer to HK as a language of change because it embodies all the elements necessary to facilitate and accelerate positive change in the individuals who experience it. HK does not diagnose or label. Please respect the context in which I present this extraordinary and very effective discipline It works on the simple premise that if it stresses you to do something (winning), you are not going to do it well.

Please set aside your prejudices, beliefs and judgments and do your best to keep an open mind. HK is a little different twist on psychology. This discipline was created with the intention of allowing you to help yourself facilitate and accelerate positive changes that will immeasurably improve the quality of your competitive performances, as well as your personal life.

There is a part of you that dramatically influences every aspect of your beingness and the experiences you create. It is known your Mind.

The Mind

When you set a goal to do something (like winning), one of two things will happen. You will either succeed or fail. What determines your success or failure is the information contained in your Mind. This stored information is the information you will use while attempting to accomplish your goal.

If the information in your Mind supports you in successfully completing your goal, the accomplishment of your goal will be easy and effortless. However, if the information in your Mind does not support you in successfully accomplishing your goal, the accomplishment of your goal will be very difficult and require a tremendous amount of effort.

The Mind is generally thought to be the seat of consciousness. It is made up of every aspect of our being. There are many philosophies that view the Mind in a way that has created numerous fragments, i.e., the spiritual mind, the emotional mind, the etheric mind, etc. I found all these subdivisions of the Mind to be very confusing.

In HK I rely upon the very old axiomatic metaphysical concept known as "cause and effect." Several of the theories that support cause and effect are, "for every action there is an equal and opposite reaction;" "water seeks it own level;" and "what goes around, comes around."

When we deal with the Mind we are dealing with something we cannot see. Although I cannot see an athlete's Mind, I can see the experiences that Mind is creating. For instance, if I am working with a professional golfer who cannot make the cut, I must assume that he has information stored in his Mind to support him missing the cut, or he would be doing something else.

It is important to note that your Mind supports you in everything you do. If you are missing the cut during a golf tournament, your Mind is supporting you, and it is doing so based upon information it has stored in its memory banks relating to making the cut. Your physical body is merely acting out (i.e., missing the cut) based upon this stored information, and it does it automatically and below your level of conscious awareness.

The same thing happens when you engage in a particular activity. Your physical body automatically acts out based upon information obtained from the subconscious part of your morphic field relating to everything from the kinds of intimate relationships you will experience, to the amount of money you will earn as an athlete in a lifetime.

To understand cause and effect, you must first understand that before anything physically happens in your life, it must first start as a thought. So, if you want to change the undesirable experiences you are creating, you must change the thoughts that are responsible for creating those undesirable experiences. This book will show you how to do it.

Every experience you create responds by corresponding. The professional golfer's experience (missing the cut) is responding by corresponding to the information stored in his Subconscious Mind relating to making the cut.

The intention of HK is to provide you with a resource that will allow you to create positive change and help you remove the psychological blockages preventing you from winning with more consistency. Before I explain how this is accomplished, it is important to establish a context and foundation whereby all the contributing factors to this performance phenomenon may be examined and understood.

It is noteworthy to point out that in HK all we are dealing with is information. For instance, although an emotion is something we can feel, it is stored in the Mind as information.

The Mind has two parts. The Conscious Mind, and the Subconscious Mind.

The Conscious Mind

The Conscious Mind is known as the "knower" because it has the ability to be aware of itself. It has the capacity to be aware of what it is thinking and feeling in the normal waking state. It also has the ability to know what it is doing and why. One of the major functions of the Conscious Mind is its use of volition. Volition is defined as, "the act of using the will; exercise of the will as in deciding what to do; a conscious or deliberate decision of choices thus made."

You are where you are in your life right now as a direct result of the choices you have made using the volitional part of your Conscious Mind. The Conscious Mind provides us with short-term memory and can only focus on one thing at a time. The Conscious Mind uses the five senses; sight, hearing, smell, taste and touch, to collect information which allows it to experience awareness.

The Conscious Mind uses this collected information to formulate your self-image, your prejudices, and your belief system. The most important function of the Conscious Mind is that it exercises its volitional capabilities by allowing us to set goals. The information collected by the Conscious Mind will influence the formulation and successful completion of the goals you set throughout your life.

So, what happens when the Conscious Mind, using its volition, decides to engage in some particular activity like competition? Well, it types out a mental memo of instructions and sends it to the Subconscious Mind.

The Subconscious Mind

When you engage in a particular activity, like tennis. it is the responsibility of your Conscious Mind to decide the nature of the activity. Your Conscious Mind will send instructions to your Subconscious Mind, "Send me all the information you have relating to tennis."

If the information accessed from your Subconscious Mind relating to tennis is supportive in nature, you will perform the activity easily and efficiently. However, if the information accessed from your Subconscious Mind is not supportive or contradicts the goal set by your Conscious Mind, your tennis related activities will become very difficult and require a tremendous amount of effort.

The Subconscious Mind is a part of the Mind known as the "doer" because it merely does what it is programmed to do. Unlike the Conscious Mind, the Subconscious Mind does not have the capacity to exercise volition or choice, it simply "does."

The Subconscious Mind acts out through the physical body and uses information it has stored in its memory banks relating to the particular activity. This "acting out" is done instantaneously and automatically. This stored information arrived into the Subconscious Mind through the Conscious Mind using the five senses (sight, hearing, smell, taste, and touch).

To more fully understand this subconscious acting out phenomenon, remember when you were a child learning how to tie your shoes? At first it required a tremendous amount of time and concentration. Now, you do it without consciously thinking because it has become a subconscious act. The same thing happens when you engage in competition. Your physical body automatically acts out based upon information obtained from your Subconscious Mind relating to everything aspect of the competition.

Your Subconscious Mind is a storage facility for all information that enters through the Conscious Mind. The one important feature to note about the Subconscious Mind is that when it is storing information it is impersonal. It doesn't say, "I am not going to store this experience because it was a bad experience." IT STORES EVERYTHING!

The Subconscious Mind also provides us with long-term memory, and is where our belief system is housed. If, for instance, you have information (belief) stored that you can only win 10% of the tennis matches you play, your physical body will reciprocate by only allowing you to win 10% of your matches. It has no other choice but to use the information available. Your Subconscious Mind will continue to do it until you change the information.

Additionally, the Subconscious Mind does not have a sense of humor and cannot distinguish between something real or imagined. If you don't believe me, try telling someone who has a fear of heights that they have nothing to be afraid of. You can clearly see how powerful our beliefs are, and that they have a tremendous influence, both positive and negative, over the decisions we make throughout our lives.

The Subconscious Mind can be likened to the hard drive of your computer with one notable exception. When using a computer, you have the option of saving or erasing the information on your screen. Every piece of information that enters the Subconscious Mind is stored for future use.

Your Conscious Mind will eventually use this subconsciously stored information when it engages in an activity that corresponds to the information in storage. The Subconscious Mind will provide the Conscious Mind with whatever information it has available. The information can be supportive or non-supportive in nature.

When subconsciously accessed information is non-supportive, the physical body will manifest stress. For example, let's say you are a NBA player and you set a goal at the beginning of the year to score 20 points a game, and the information you have stored subconsciously is that you are only capable of scoring 12 points a game. Your physical body will immediately manifest stress.

Your Subconscious Mind is basically telling your Conscious Mind, "I do not have information stored to support you in scoring 20 points a game, however, I do have information stored to support you in scoring 12 points a game." The end result, you will score 12 points a game.

WHENEVER THERE IS CONFLICT BETWEEN THE CONSCIOUS MIND AND THE SUBCONCIOUS MIND, THAT CONFLICT WILL ALWAYS MANIFEST IN THE PHYSICAL BODY AS STRESS!

It's as if the Conscious Mind and the Subconscious Mind are not on the same page. When stress is present in the physical body, it will always weaken the body. It is when your physical body is in this weakened or stressed state during competition that you will make an uncharacteristic mental error that will adversely affect your performance during the competition.

It's as if your physical body goes on red alert because the information in the Conscious Mind (20 points a game) does not match the information accessed from the Subconscious Mind (12 points a game). The Subconscious Mind, acting out through the physical body, will do everything in its power to sabotage any attempt by the NBA player to score 20 points a game.

You must understand that your Subconscious Mind is not being vindictive, it is simply saying, "My hands are tied. I would love to help you score 20 points a game, but I don't have that information in storage to support you."

There is a very integral component of the Mind that gets involved when the Conscious and the

Subconscious Mind interact. It is known to as the Critical Factor.

The Critical Factor

After information enters the Conscious Mind, it is reviewed prior to storage in the Subconscious Mind. The responsibility for this task belongs to a component of the Mind known as the Critical Factor. The Critical Factor literally criticizes or reviews information that comes into conscious awareness.

After its review, the Critical Factor must make a decision regarding the disposition of the information. The Critical Factor has two options. It can either store the information, or reject it. Everyone knows that the color of the sky is blue, but suppose I told you that the color of the sky was red.

When that statement enters your Conscious Mind, your Critical Factor will stop it momentarily and says something to the effect, "Let me check the information I have in subconscious storage relating to the color of the sky." The Critical Factor checks and discovers that the information stored in the Subconscious Mind indicates that the color of the sky is blue. The Critical Factor proceeds to reject the statement, "The sky is red."

Let's assume that you are a major league pitcher and you set a goal at the beginning of the season to win 20 games that year. Your Conscious Mind will send instructions to your Subconscious Mind, "Send me all the information you have stored relating to winning 20 game this year?"

Your Critical Factor will stop this information before it hits the Subconscious Mind and say something to the effect, "Let's see what kind of information we have in subconscious storage relating to winning 20 games this year."

The Critical Factor checks and discovers that the information stored indicates that your yearly game winning threshold is at 12, and proceeds to reject the statement.

It's as if the Critical Factor instructs the pitcher's Subconscious Mind to go on "red alert" and proceeds to sabotage any attempt at winning more than 12 games for the year because the Subconscious Mind does not have the information to support the pitcher in willing 20 games.

It is absolutely crucial that you understand the role your Critical Factor plays in sabotaging your success as an athlete. It is not being vindictive, but rather impersonal. It is basically saying, "I would love to support you in winning 20 games this year, but I just don't have the information stored to support you in doing that." When you change the subconsciously stored information, you change the experience.

Imagine the Critical Factor as a guard, and that it is guarding all information coming into and leaving the Mind. How do you change this information? How do you change subconsciously stored information preventing you from winning with more consistency? In order to change subconsciously stored information, you must achieve Critical Factor Bypass.

Critical Factor Bypass

Critical Factor Bypass occurs when new information is allowed to bypass the Critical Factor of the Mind in an effort to change old information stored in the Subconscious Mind. HK can achieve Critical Factor Bypass, which enables you to literally change subconsciously stored information.

Using HK to achieve Critical Factor Bypass allows us to accelerate change for the athletes who experience it. In order to more fully understand Critical Factor Bypass, we must first look to the advertising industry.

On many occasions advertising agencies will send sales copy to a psychologist, and ask, "Will this copy achieve Critical Factor Bypass for our product or service?" The ad agencies know that if they can achieve Critical Factor Bypass on anyone who hears or sees their commercials, their chances of selling their product or service are greatly enhanced.

They carefully choose the people who star in these commercials, carefully choose the wording, and carefully choose the scenarios. How can they motivate someone to buy their product or service? One way to do it is using fear in the form of authority figures. It cannot be done blatantly. It must be subtle.

Have you ever noticed that many ad agencies will use policemen, judges, doctors, or firemen in their commercials? All these professions represent authority figures and the ad agencies know that when a policeman tells you to do something, you normally do it without question. You do what you are told because the policeman, as an authority figure, was able to achieve Critical Factor Bypass.

Another very subtle tactic ad agencies will use to create Critical Factor Bypass is race and gender. I once saw a print ad that contained a Caucasian, an African-American, an Asian, an older gentleman, an older woman, a young man, and a young woman. They covered a lot of bases with that ad., and it is all done subjectively, or below your level of conscious awareness.

Sometimes the ad agencies will appeal to your emotions. I am certain you have seen the Michelin Tire commercial with a baby sitting in a tire. That commercial has been running for years. This particular commercial has been successful because the ad agency was able to achieve Critical Factor Bypass by using the baby to appeal to the emotions of the viewer. Babies are sweet and adorable and Michelin must be selling a lot of tires, or they would not continue to use this very effective commercial.

Some of the other tactics used by ad agencies are humor, sex and money. In fact, the next time you view or hear a commercial advertisement, ask yourself, "What are they doing in this commercial to achieve Critical Factor Bypass?" I will explain in a later chapter how we are able to achieve Critical Factor Bypass using HK so that you can clear the psychological blockages preventing you from winning with more consistency.

For now, we have examined the nuances of the Mind to include the Conscious Mind, the Subconscious Mind, the Critical Factor, and Critical Factor Bypass. The Mind must act out through the physical body and it does this using your Brain.

The Brain

Although the Mind is the decision maker, it is the brain's responsibility to physically carry out those instructions. The brain is a part of the Central Nervous System composed of approximately 10 billion nerve cells. Each cell is linked to one another, and together they are responsible for the control of all functions in the physical body. The brain disseminates these instructions throughout the physical body using information provided by the Mind in the form of electrical impulses.

The brain is an organ consisting of three major components. The Left Hemisphere, The Right Hemisphere and the Corpus Callosum. Although these three components are integral, they each have very specific and different functions, and two of these components can function independently should the need arise. The Left Hemisphere of the brain controls the right side of the physical body, while the Right Hemisphere controls the left side.

We need only look at a stroke victim to understand this phenomenon. Notice that in the majority of the cases only one side of the body is paralyzed. That's because the hemisphere of the brain on the opposite side of the affected area was so severely damaged during the stroke that it manifested as paralysis.

The corresponding side of the physical body is not receiving electrical impulses (information) from the damaged hemisphere resulting in partial or total paralysis. There are degrees of dysfunction between the brain and the physical body after a stroke, and that total paralysis represents the extreme.

Since the Left and Right Hemispheres of your brain can function independently and have their own responsibilities, they need some way to communicate. This is accomplished using the Corpus Callosum. The Corpus Callosum is a band of nerve fibers that connect the Left and Right Hemispheres of your brain. The hemispheres share and exchange information (electrical impulses) that will eventually be disseminated to your physical body.

What I realized in my research in working with athletes was that the hemispheres of your brain have a tendency to weaken or switch off. When one hemisphere is switched off, the opposite hemisphere will dominate.

For instance, if your Left Hemisphere is switched off, your Right Hemisphere will dominate and dramatically influence your activity. The hemispheres of the brain are continually influenced by and are reacting to, stimuli in your immediate external environment.

The brain does basically three things. It processes (learns), stores, and disseminates information. What kind of information? That would be any and all information relating to pictures, sounds, fragrances, culinary data, and touch. All three of the major components of your brain come into play when the brain is exercising these functions. Let's first examine the Left Hemisphere of the brain.

The Left Hemisphere

When the Left Hemisphere of your brain processes (learns) information, it only understands words, language and numbers. That's because the Left Hemisphere processes information sequentially, or one piece at a time. The Left Hemisphere is one-dimensional, and can only focus on one thing at a time. The Left Hemisphere controls the right side of your physical body and it accomplishes this by sending information in the form of electrical impulses.

When the Left Hemisphere of your brain weakens or switches off, during the processing or learning stage, it's as if a short circuit occurs in the electrical field in your physical body, and the incoming information never reaches the hemisphere of the brain that is switched off. Incoming information will only store in the hemisphere that is switched on.

For instance, if your Right Hemisphere is switched off while your brain is learning, the incoming information will store in your Left Hemisphere. Now, because there was no information stored in your Right Hemisphere, when it's time for your brain to disseminate the information to you at some point in the future, you will only receive information from your Left Hemisphere. It's as if you are only getting half the information.

When the Left Hemisphere of your brain stores information, it will only store sequential information such as words, language and numbers. It will store information that is logical and organized. In other words, the information stored in the Left Hemisphere must be structured.

When the brain disseminates information to your physical body, the Left and Right Hemispheres deal with different and specific information. The Left Hemisphere of the brain provides the physical body with the following information, attributes and qualities:

Logic, action, decision making, critical, one-dimensional, mechanical, compulsive, doubt, cautious, judgmenta, hard working, limitation, shame, rational, stoic, organization, reasoning, rules, hard, cold, specificity, structure, boundaries, rigidity, opinionated,
intense, impersona, unfeeling, introverted, controlled, predictable, restricted, precise, serious, conservative, quiet, intolerant, auditory, scientific, temporal (the now), fearful and finite.

When you engage in an activity and the Right Hemisphere of your brain is weak or switched off, your physical body is only receiving information, or a majority of the information, from your Left Hemisphere. This causes you to become left-brain dominant while you are engaged in that particular activity. This anomaly results in you exhibiting one or more of the personality traits listed above.

For example, a left-brain dominant individual is introverted, dresses very conservatively, and is extremely critical of others. Whenever you encounter people who are very critical of others they are most critical of themselves because by criticizing others they are attempting to redirect attention away from themselves by putting the focus on others' mistakes rather than their own. It's as if they do it to extremes.

I believe this switching off anomaly is one reason that science speculates that we only use 10% of our brain. Now let's examine the Right Hemisphere of the brain.

The Right Hemisphere

When the Right Hemisphere of your brain processes information, it only understands movement and pictures. That's because the Right Hemisphere is spatial and can process information collectively rather than sequentially. This collectiveness allows it to process large amounts of information at one time. It can only process non-sequential information.

For instance, if you were looking at a picture of a landscape with your Left Hemisphere, you would have to look at every piece of the picture individually because the Left Hemisphere processes information sequentially. You cannot see the whole picture if you are only looking at one piece. The collective capabilities of the Right Hemisphere allows you to see the whole picture, while the Left Hemisphere provides you with the capacity to structure the collective information in the form of discernible images.

When we examine this phenomenon during the learning stage of your development, we can clearly see how the hemispheres of the brain influence how you learn. Let's look at an elementary school student named Harold. He is learning to read the sentence, "See Jack jump." If Harold had the Right Hemisphere of his brain weak or switched off while reading this sentence, his Left Hemisphere would dominate.

Now, keeping in mind that the Left Hemisphere processes information sequentially, Harold's Left Hemisphere will know and understand the words <u>see</u>, <u>Jack</u>, and <u>jump</u> individually. However, because his Right Hemisphere is weak or switched off, he will have difficulty achieving total comprehension. In order for that to happen, he would have to send the information from his Left Hemisphere, via the corpus callosum, to the Right Hemisphere, and request additional information such as a visual of a boy jumping. With both hemispheres of his brain participating in the learning process, Harold will achieve total comprehension, no matter what he is learning.

When the brain disseminates information to your physical body, the Right and Left Hemispheres deal with different and specific information. The Right Hemisphere of the brain provides the physical body with the following information, attributes and qualities:

Feelings, emotions, relaxation, beliefs, creativity, flexibility, physical movement, tolerance, visualization, artistic, spatial, self-esteem, forgiveness, no boundaries, unstructured, generalizations, procrastination, compassion, optimism, passivity, funny, unreasonable, loud, expressive, foolish, passion, charming, intuition, love, uncontrollable, multi-dimensional, imagination, addictions, lazy, laid back, open-minded, unorganized and infinite.

When the Left Hemisphere of your brain is weak or switched off, the Right Hemisphere will dominate your activities, from your decision making to your personality. Since your physical body is only receiving information from the Right Hemisphere of your brain, you will exhibit one or more of the above listed personality traits and attributes. Again, it's as if your behavior becomes extreme.

If you have ever seen a golfer bend his putter in half and throw it into the lake because he missed a birdie putt, or how many times have you been very passionate about a particular cause? It is during these times when the Right Hemisphere of your brain was dominating your thinking.

The objective in HK is to help you switch on both hemispheres of your brain in relationship to a thought, statement or action. Having both hemispheres of your brain switched on insures that you will have access to information such as judgment, analysis and structure (Left Hemisphere), as well as creativity, imagination and intuition (Right Hemisphere). With both hemispheres of your brain providing your physical body with information, you will experience total balance in your competitive as well as your personal life.

A great analogy for explaining hemispheric balance is water. The Right Hemisphere can be likened to boiling hot water, while the Left Hemisphere is ice-cold water. By themselves, their temperatures are very uncomfortable. However, when you mix them together, you get a warm, comfortable and balanced temperature. When both hemispheres of your brain are switched on, you enter a mental space that athletes refer to as "The Zone."

Another salient difference between the hemispheres worthy of note is that the Left Hemisphere deals with "old" information, while the Right Hemisphere deals with "new" information. This influences how the hemispheres of your brain will handle a specific task. Let's assume that you have just purchased something that requires assembly.

The Left Hemisphere of your brain will approach the task by saying something like, "Where are the instructions to this thing (?); I can't put this together without the directions!" Remember that because the Left Hemisphere is using "old" information, it is basically saying, "Show me the way some else did it, then I can do it."

Conversely, the Right Hemisphere will approach that same task by saying, "Hey, even if we don't have the instructions, let's try putting it together anyway." That's because the Right Hemisphere is providing the physical body with "new" information in the form of "creativity," and will figure it out eventually. The Right Hemisphere will risk (no instructions), while the Left Hemisphere will tend to play it safe (must have instructions).

For example, let's assume you are a football coach and you are in the 4th quarter with the score tied and 10 seconds left on the clock. You are trailing by 3 points and it's 4th and goal on the 3 yard line. You call your last time out. If you are a left brain dominant coach (right hemisphere switched off), you will have a tendency to play it safe. You will kick the field goal. If you are right brain dominant (left hemisphere switched off), you will have a tendency to risk. You will go for the touchdown.

When you can compete with both hemispheres of your brain strong or switched on, you will achieve a level of performance that most competitors just dream of. With access to structure, judgment and organization (Left Hemisphere), and creativity, intuition and imagination (Right Hemisphere), every decision you make supports you in winning.

When I do private sessions with athletes using HK, it is imperative that I know what activity is taking place in the physical body in relationship to a statement, thought or action. This is accomplished using Muscle Testing.

Muscle Testing

There are three vital pieces of information that muscle testing allows me to obtain in relationship to a statement, thought or action. First, muscle testing allows me to determine whether the physical body is weak or strong.

Secondly, muscle testing allows me to determine the condition of the hemispheres of the brain. Thirdly, muscle testing allows me to post test and validate that the stress has been cleared from the physical body.

Muscle testing is a technique that has been widely used in the alternative health field for years and has been used in a variety of applications. I use muscle testing to determine whether stress is present in your physical body relating to a statement, thought or action.

Since your physical body is merely acting out based upon information contained in your Subconscious Mind, muscle testing allows me to tap into that subconsciously stored information. It's a form of bio-feedback.

In his book "Switching On," Dr. Paul Dennison defines muscle testing as:

"Muscle testing is the art of isolating and testing one muscle at a time in order to determine if it is 'weak' or 'strong' relative to the strength of the individual being tested."

There are forty-two muscle groups in the physical body. In HK, I muscle test the deltoid muscle. The deltoid is the larger triangular muscle of the shoulder, which raises the arm away from the side. If you held your right arm straight out from your side, parallel to the ground, and lifted your arm upward from that point, it is the deltoid muscle that allows you to execute that movement.

When I muscle test someone I will ask them to:

1. Stand with weight evenly distributed on both feet;
2. I have the subject hold his left or right arm straight out or parallel to the ground;
3. I face the subject standing in front of the outstretched arm;
4. I ask the subject to look straight ahead and extend the fingers of his outstretched arm so that they are parallel to the ground;
5. I place my left hand on the subject's left shoulder for support;
6. I place my right hand, using only two fingers (index and middle fingers) on top of the subject's outstretched arm between the elbow and wrist;
7. The subject is now ready to be muscle tested;
8. I will ask the subject to resist upwards slightly, towards the sky, while I apply about 2 ounces of pressure downward towards the ground. This allows both the subject and I to get a feel for the muscle test.

The key to muscle testing effectively is 2-2-2. Use two fingers, apply two ounces of pressure, and hold for two seconds. There are two possible responses to a muscle test. Strong, or weak.

A strong muscle test indicates that my downward pressing motion was unable to budge your arm. A strong muscle test also indicates that there was no stress present in your physical body relating to the statement, thought or action for which I muscle tested.

A weak muscle test indicates that you were unable to resist my downward pressure, and could not hold your arm parallel to the ground. A weak muscle test is evidence that stress was present in your physical body relating to the statement, thought or action for which I muscle tested.

What does a strong vs a weak muscle test tell me, if anything? Well, if I had had a coach make the statement, "I consistently win 90% of the games I coach," the strong muscle test signifies that the coach's physical body would totally support him in winning 90% of the games he coaches. The absence of stress in the coach's physical body indicates that there is information stored in his Subconscious Mind that would support him in winning 90% of his games.

On the other hand, had the coach muscle tested weak to the statement relating to a 90% winning percentage, the weak muscle test indicates the presence of stress in his physical body relating to the statement. It basically stressed the coach to say, "I consistently win 90% of the games I coach."

The weak muscle test tells me that the information stored in the coach's Subconscious Mind would not support him in winning 90% of his games. A weak muscle test is the physical body's way of saying, "I am not doing that because I do not have information stored in my memory banks to support the activity, or that the information I have stored contradicts whatever it is you want to do (90% winning percentage)."

The second piece of information I can obtain using muscle testing is the condition of the Right or Left Hemispheres of your brain in relationship to a statement, thought or action. For instance, when checking the condition of your Left Hemisphere, I merely touch the left side of your head and muscle test.

If I record a strong muscle test, the hemisphere is switched on. If I record a weak muscle test, your Left Hemisphere is switched off. I would do likewise to check the condition of the Right Hemisphere.

Checking the hemispheres of the brain allows me to determine how you would function while engaged in the activity for which we are muscle testing. For example, if I muscle tested you for winning the next cortest you entered, and you had your Left Hemisphere switched on and your Right Hemisphere switched off, your Left Hemisphere would dominate your approach to the goal.

You would exhibit the personality traits and attributes listed under the Left Hemisphere of the brain. You will try to use "old" information. For instance, what did I do last week to win; what did I do the week before; Etc. It's as if you are walking through a mental revolving door.

You keep creating the same experience because you are using the same information from your Left Hemisphere. Without the participation of your Right Hemisphere you would be lacking information such as intuition, creativity and imagination.

Thirdly, and most importantly, muscle testing allows me to validate, through post testing, that the stress relating to the subject matter has been cleared from your physical body. If I have you say "I will win XYZ contest," and you muscle test weak, and then have you say it again, and you muscle test strong, something obviously changed in your physical body and the way it reacted to the statement.

In HK, muscle testing allows me access your Subconscious Mind. If subconsciously stored information is to be changed, it must be done subconsciously. Muscle testing allows me to inferentially (indirectly) access information from your Subconscious Mind using your physical body. That's because your Mind and your physical body are integral and mirror each other. What affects your Mind affects your physical body.

When the physical body is in a weakened state, it is engaged in a sabotage state. Muscle testing allows me to interpret the language used by the physical body to communicate this sabotage state, and that language is Stress.

Stress

Taber's Cyclopedic Medical Dictionary defines stress as, "...the result produced when a structure, system or organism is acted upon by forces that disrupt equilibrium or produce strain...the term denotes the physical and psychological forces that are experienced by individuals." Stress has an absolutely pervasive effect on the physical body, and the prolonged presence of stress in the body can manifest pathologically (disease).

When stress is present in the physical body, it creates a myriad of physiological changes. Some of the more salient physical reactions to stress are:

* Increase in the rate and force of heartbeat;
* A rise in systolic blood pressure;
* Sweating of the palms and hands;
* Dilation of the pupils;
* Decreased digestion;
* Blood distribution from less to more active organs;
* Increased blood glucose (hyperglycemia);
* Etc;

Can you imagine having to make a three foot putt with a left to right break to win the U.S. Open with all this activity going on in your body? When stress is present in the physical body, it interrupts the electrical signals between your brain and your muscles causing your body to weaken. It also disrupts your thought processes. When your body is in this weakened state it is attempting to sabotage your activity because there is a conflict between your Conscious and Subconscious Mind.

When your body is in this weakened state during competition you will make an uncharacteristic mental error that will adversely affect the outcome of the game. This sabotaging phenomenon is so subtle that you will be totally unaware that you are doing it because it is all happening subjectively or subconsciously. That is to say it is happening below your level of conscious awareness.

Please remember that it is not what you are doing, but where you are doing it. Here's why. Take a 12 inch wide plank and connect it to two buildings 5 feet off the ground and ask someone to walk across it. No problem.

Now, take that same 12 inch wide plank up to the 30th floor and ask that same person to walk across it. I guarantee you will get a different response. The stress response is significantly higher up on the 30th floor versus 5 feet off the ground. It is not what you are doing, but where you are doing it.

The presence of stress in your physical body adversely affects you mentally by weakening or switching off one or both hemispheres of your brain. When stress is present in your physical body during competition, something is motivating your body to manifest stress. That something is a Synthesizing Event.

Synthesizing Events

A synthesizing event is created when the emotions from a traumatic experience actually synthesize (comes together) with the information as it is being stored in the Subconscious Mind. This synthesized information remains stored and dormant in the Subconscious Mind until the Conscious Mind engages in some activity relative to the stored information or event.

Once the Conscious Mind accesses this synthesized information, it will manifest in your physical body as stress. One of the best analogies I have ever heard in describing, synthesizing events is to imagine that you have just purchased a brand new boat. The hull of this boat is clean and spotless. As you travel on water, barnacles will attach themselves to the hull.

The more barnacles that attach to the hull, the slower the boat will travel, until the boat accumulates so many barnacles it stops all together. Synthesizing events are like barnacles that have attached themselves to the hulls of our lives. If you accumulate enough barnacles they may manifest as a nervous breakdown, or some chronic illness.

The barnacle analogy is likened to psychological blockages that people carry around with them for years, and it adversely affects every aspect of their lives. When you accumulate too many synthesizing events you will more than likely have to go on some form of medication (anti-depressants, etc) just to make it through the day.

What's responsible for creating synthesizing events? Trauma! Webster's defines trauma as, "1. A bodily injury or shock; 2. An emotional shock, often having lasting psychic effects." As you can clearly see, trauma can be experienced both physically and mentally, and can range from mild to severe. The physical trauma from dislocating a shoulder during competition, for example, will heal with time.

However, the mental (emotional) trauma from the injury may stay in your physical body for years. How about this scenario? You are a basketball coach coaching a championship game with a 1-point lead and 2 seconds left on the clock, and a player on the other team throws a Hail Mary ball and it goes in and your team loses. The resulting emotional trauma from that loss stored in your Subconscious Mind as a synthesizing event and may adversely affect your coaching for years.

There are two types of synthesizing events. The initial synthesizing event and the subsequent synthesizing event. The following analogy explains. Suppose you had a fear of heights. There was a first time you experienced that fear and it is referred to as the initial synthesizing event because it was the first time the synthesizing dynamics came into play relating to the experience.

That synthesized information is stored in your Subconscious Mind, and will remain dormant until you go near a high place again. Once this happens, your Conscious Mind sends instructions to your Subconscious Mind, "Send me all the information you have stored relating to being near a high place."

The stored information from the first experience comes up, and since an emotion has synthesized with the information, it comes up as well. Your first reaction is, "Let's get away from this ledge!" The second experience created a subsequent synthesizing event. And, you will have no idea why you have a fear of heights because it is happening subjectively, or below your level of conscious awareness.

Once you have left harms' way and are in a safe place, the initial synthesizing event is once again stored in your Subconscious Mind, and the subsequent synthesizing event is stored for the first time. Now you have two subconsciously stored pieces of information (or experiences) to support your fear of heights, and so on.

Imagine an onion. Its center represents the kind of competitor you have the potential to become. Over the years you have accumulated layers of synthesizing events preventing you from realizing that potential.

If you don't get rid of them at some point your onion will continue to grow and you will carry these psychological blockages with you from competition to competition. In order to access the center of your onion (your true potential to win consistently), these layers of synthesizing events must be peeled away, and that is exactly what HK and this program will help you do.

I once had a PGA Tour player I was working with ask me, "Why is it I can shoot a 64 in the pro-am and on the next day using the same equipment, playing on the same golf course, I shoot a 74?

I simply explained the 12" plank analogy to him and told him it is not what you are doing, but where you are doing it.

It is my belief that 95% of all synthesizing events are stored in your Subconscious Mind during a period in your childhood development known as the Egocentric Stage.

The Egocentric Stage

There is a period in your childhood known as the egocentric stage, and it occurs between conception and 7 to 8 years of age. It was during this stage in your development when most of the synthesizing events were stored in your Subconscious Mind.

Webster's defines egocentricity as, "Regarding the self or the individual as the center of all things; Having little or no regard for interests or feelings other than one's own; Self-centered." The egocentric child is so self-centered that the first thought they have when something goes wrong in their lives is, "What did I do wrong?"

If you ask a three-year-old boy if he has a brother, he will answer yes. If you ask that same three-year-old boy if his brother has a brother, he will answer no. That's because the egocentric child cannot objectify his experience, he can only experience.

It's as if he cannot see himself. The reason for this phenomenon is that the egocentric child's Mind does not possess a critical factor. Remember that the critical factor allows your Mind to accept or reject incoming information passing through your Conscious Mind.

Without the capacity to criticize incoming information, the egocentric child's Subconscious Mind stores everything! At age 7 or 8 the child's critical factor starts kicking in. During the child's teen years, it is operating at full capacity because teenagers know everything and adults know nothing. After the teen years, our criticalness starts reversing and by middle age, most of us experience a softening of our attitudes and come to realize that criticism was all a waste of good energy to begin with.

The absence of the critical factor also denies the egocentric child the capacity to rationalize. You cannot rationalize with someone who is incapable of objectifying their experiences. Some of the other anomalies associated with the egocentric child:

*   Absolutize – You either love me or you hate me;
*   Personalize   -   Takes   everything personally;
*   Idealize their role models – If dad says I'm stupid, it must be true;
*   Self-blame – What did I do wrong;
*   Shame – There must be something wrong with me;

Children have very limited resources when dealing with trauma. The only way they know how to deal with trauma is to block it out. They accomplish this by switching off one or both hemispheres of their brains depending on the severity of the trauma. This switching off will influence the decisions they make for the rest of their lives.

In the 1980's John Bradshaw brought to light much information relating to dysfunctional families. In a dysfunctional family, the members are simply not getting their needs met. What kinds of needs? The need to be loved, nurtured and respected. It was during this stage in our development that we accepted beliefs about ourselves that simply were not true. We accepted beliefs that we were not smart enough, good enough, tall enough, thin enough, this enough or that enough.

If you have ever accepted a belief about yourself that you weren't good enough IT WASN'T TRUE! Please know you accepted that belief during a time in your development when you did not possess a Critical Factor and you were incapable of objectifying and rejecting that information or belief.

So, what kind of a family environment would produce a functional child or adult? The following quote is from a book titled Trauma and Recovery by Dr. Judith Herman that will provide you with profound insight:

"The developing child's positive sense of self depends upon a caretaker's benign use of power. When a parent, who is so much more powerful than a child, nevertheless shows some regard for that child's individuality and dignity, that child feels valued and respected; he develops self-esteem. He also develops autonomy, that is, a sense of his own separateness within a relationship. He learns to control and regulate his own bodily functions and to form and express his own point of view."

Wouldn't it have been nice to have been raised in this environment? The truth is that 99% of all families are dysfunctional. This dysfunction leaves most children who experience it filled with shame and doubt. Dr. Herman continues:

"Shame is a response to helplessness, the violation of bodily integrity, and the indignity suffered in the eyes of another person. Doubt reflects the inability to maintain one's own separate point of view while remaining in connection with others. In the aftermath of traumatic events, survivors doubt both others and themselves."

If you show a child respect, he learns to respect himself and others. If a child is shown disrespect, it traumatizes him and creates a synthesizing event. As that child is creating a self-image, the synthesizing event will no doubt play a significant role in determining how that child will perceive himself. The switching off the hemispheres will cause the child to become either left brained or right brained dominant.

Here is an extraordinary example of how things we learn about ourselves during the egocentric stage of our development stay with us the rest of our lives. One day a teacher asked her students to list the names of the other students in the room on two sheets of paper, leaving a space between each name. Then she told them to think of the nicest thing they could say about each of their classmates and write it down. It took the remainder of the class period to finish their assignment, and as the students left the room, each one handed in the papers.

That Saturday, the teacher wrote down the name of each student on a separate sheet of paper, and listed what everyone else had said about that individual. On Monday she gave each student his or her list. Before long, the entire class was smiling. 'Really?' she heard whispered. "I never knew that I meant anything to anyone!" and, "I didn't know others liked me so much," were most of the comments.

No one ever mentioned those papers in class again. She never knew if the students discussed them after class or with their parents, but it didn't matter. The exercise had accomplished its purpose. The students were happy with themselves and one another. That group of students moved on.

Several years later, one of the students was killed in Viet Nam and his teacher attended the funeral of that special student. She had never seen a serviceman in a military coffin before. He looked so handsome, so mature. The church was packed with his friends. One by one those who loved him took a last walk by the coffin. The teacher was the last one to bless the coffin.

As she stood there, one of the soldiers who acted as pallbearer came up to her. "Were you Mark's math teacher?" he asked. She nodded, "Yes." Then he said, "Mark talked about you a lot." After the funeral, most of Mark's former classmates went together to a luncheon. Mark's mother and father were there, obviously waiting to speak with his teacher. "We want to show you something," his father said, taking a wallet out of his pocket. "They found this on Mark when he was killed. We thought you might recognize it."

Opening the billfold, he carefully removed two worn pieces of notebook paper that had obviously been taped, folded and refolded many times. The teacher knew without looking that the papers were the ones on which she had listed all the good things each of Mark's classmates had said about him. 'Thank you so much for doing that," Mark's mother said, "'As you can see, Mark treasured it."

All of Mark's former classmates started to gather around. Charlie smiled rather sheepishly and said, "I still have my list. It's in the top drawer of my desk at home." Chuck's wife said, "Chuck asked me to put his in our wedding album." ' have mine too," Marilyn said, "It's in my diary." Then Vicki, another classmate, reached into her pocketbook, took out her wallet and showed her worn and frazzled list to the group. "I carry this with me at all times," Vicki said and without batting an eyelash, she continued, "I think we all saved our lists."

If you tell a 6 year old he isn't good enough, he has no way of stopping that information. It goes right into subconscious storage and will be used at some point in his future to create his self-image. If you treat that same 6 years with respect and tell him he is loved and cherished he will, likewise, store the information subconsciously and it will have a profoundly positive impact on his self-image, and he will carry it with him for the rest of his life.

Many children start their athletic careers playing youth sports during the egocentric stage of their development. If you are a coach, please be ever mindful of what to tell these children whenever you interact with them. Because they respect you, the will believe everything you tell them.

Sometimes the trauma is so severe that it causes both hemispheres of the brain to weaken or switch off. This creates a condition known as Dissociation.

Dissociation

As I had mentioned earlier, children do not have a lot of options when dealing with trauma. Children deal with it by blocking it out. They accomplish this by switching off one of both hemispheres of their brains depending upon the severity of the trauma. When both hemispheres of the brain switch off it creates a condition known as dissociation.

Dissociation occurs when specific mental functions become separated (or dissociated) from the mainstream of consciousness and, as a consequence, are lost to the individual's awareness and voluntary control. When an athlete, for instance, dissociates during the decision making process in a game, he does not have access to creativity or intuition (Right Hemisphere switched off), nor is there structure to his thinking (Left Hemisphere switched off).

This condition results in the player experiencing an uncharacteristic mental error at a crucial point during the competition. It will cause a pitcher to walk in the winning run in the bottom of the 9th inning, or cause a wide receiver to drop a pass thrown right into his hands.

It's as if you are totally disconnected from your body. There is a way to help you keep both hemispheres of their brains switched on during competition and it involves achieving Critical Factor Bypass. This is accomplished with the use of the HK Performance Trigger.

The HK Performance Trigger

We now know that when you experience a traumatic encounter (losing a close game), the emotions from that trauma will synthesize with the information stored in his Subconscious Mind and adversely affect you in future competitions. In order to clear the synthesizing event(s), a desynthesis must occur. In order to neutralize the synthesizing event, I employ the HK Performance Trigger.

The HK Performance Trigger creates a medium to facilitate the release of trauma and all associated emotions connected to that trauma from your Subconscious Mind manifesting as stress in your physical body.

In other words, the intention of the HK Performance Trigger is to sever the emotional trauma from the information stored in your Subconscious Mind creating the stress in your physical body. It works because "energy follows intention."

The HK Performance Trigger is used to create Critical Factor Bypass so that you may change the subconsciously stored information preventing you from becoming a more consistent winner. Every time you use the HK Performance Trigger you are changing information on a subconscious level.

Or, to put it another way, you are peeling the onion. Your objective is to get to the center of the onion because that is where you will find your true potential to become a more consistent winner. The more you do something the better you get at it. So, the more you use the HK Performance Trigger, the stronger and more effective it becomes.

The HK Performance Trigger was designed to help you peel away the psychological blockages preventing you from playing your best during competition. Now, let's show you how to use HK to clear these blockages.

The first part of this book was intended to provide you with a context that would help you understand why you are not competing up to your potential. The second part will show you how to use HK to clear those blockages and gain the maximum benefit from using this program.

You will be shown step by step:

1. How to program in the HK Performance Trigger;
2. How to use the HK Performance Trigger;
3. How to do the HK Journaling exercise;
4. How to use the Mind Mastery For Winning program;
5. The importance of setting goals.

Let's first show you how to program in the HK Performance Trigger.

Programming In The HK Performance Trigger

There are three steps to programming in the HK Performance Trigger:

Step #1: Read the following statement aloud:

"I, (state your name), now accept and integrate into my Mind and body the HK Performance Trigger which is stating, thinking or hearing the word 'relax' and touching the thumb and index fingers of both hands, to immediately and permanently neutralize all initial and subsequent synthesizing events manifesting as stress in every cell, organ and tissue of my physical body, and to 'switch on' the left and right hemispheres of my brain as well as my corpus callosum so that all three components function as one allowing me to always remain in present time, and to activate that part of my Mind that supports and allows me to experience and be open to receive more wealth, health, happiness, peace, joy, prosperity, safety and security in my life, and all other attributes I may require to help me experience the lifestyle of my choosing, to help me successfully accomplish all my goals, and to improve the quality of my life, and I will never interfere with the physical manifestation of all my goals, needs and desires, and every time I activate my HK Trigger it will become ten times more powerful, and allow me to switch on that part of my Mind that allows me to experience all the attributes I may require to help me win every competition in which I compete, and help me successfully accomplish all my competitive and personal goals, relating to every statement, thought and action I experience, layers one through infinity."

Step #2: Say the word "relax" and touch the thumb and index fingers of both hands, then release and open your fingers.

Step #3: Read the statement in Step #1 again. Remember to read it aloud so that you involve as many of your senses as possible. The HK Performance Trigger, which is stating or thinking the word "relax" and touching the thumb and index fingers of both hands, is now programmed into your Subconscious Mind.

The HK Performance Trigger is intended to help you stay calm, relaxed, and focused. When you can remain calm and relaxed while engaged in competition your brain functions at maximum capacity. This will provide you with the mental clarity necessary to help you create a strategy that will support you in winning. This ultimately results in more consistency in your thought processes, and the decisions you make during competition will dramatically enhance your chances of winning.

If the presence of stress in your physical body indicates that you are in a sabotage mode, then the intention of the HK Performance Trigger is to get you in a calm and relaxed state of mind during competition. When you can remain calm and relaxed while competing that is when you experience peak performance.

During this peak mental state, both your

Conscious and Subconscious Mind are on the same page. When your Conscious Mind decides to do XYZ, your Subconscious Mind will support you in doing it, and you will do it well.

The reason the HK Performance Trigger is so effective is because "energy follows intention." Remember that the more you use the trigger, the stronger it becomes. There is an excellent process we use in HK to extract information from your Subconscious Mind. It is called HK Journaling.

HK Journaling

Remember that one of the limitations of the Conscious Mind is that it can only focus on one thing at a time. If you are not winning as much as you would like, there is usually more than one thing responsible for the problem. HK Journaling allows you to bring up those problems, or the negative experiences you had during competition, one at a time, and in order of their priority.

HK Journaling entails the use of open-ended statements to access subconsciously stored information manifesting as problems during your competition. Grab a pencil and a blank piece of paper and draw a line down the center of the page. At the top of the left side of the page write the word Negative. At the top of the right side of the page write the word Positive.

Using open-ended statements, list the negative things that occurred for you during your game or match on the left side of the page. For instance, let's assume that you are a football coach and your team just lost an important conference game. (This process can be used with any sport or subject) Here is how you would document this information.

1.   One of the negative things that occurred during my last game was: We lost the game by 3 points;

2.   The second negative thing that occurred during my last game was: On 4th and goal I decided to go for it instead of kicking a field goal;

3. The third negative thing that occurred during my last game was: Etc.

After you have finished documenting all the negative things that occurred for you during your game, go to the top of the right side of the page and document all the positive things that occurred for you.

1. One of the positive things that occurred during my last game was: Our defensive strategy held the opposing team to 10 points;

2. The second positive thing that occurred during my last game was: Both running backs gained over 100 yards rushing;

3. The third positive thing that occurred during my last game was: Etc.

It is important to also focus on the positive things that occurred during your game because if you only focus on the negative that is all you will see. It reminds me of an old saying I once heard, "You are never as good as you think you are, but you are never as bad either." Looking at both negative and positive elements of your competitive performance just gives you a more balanced perspective on what's really going on for you.

As you can clearly see, the HK Journaling exercise allows you to document a tremendous amount of information regarding your performance during competition, and the problems that came up for you. If you made an uncharacteristic mental error at a crucial point in the game, something motivated you to do that. And, that something was mental, and that is what we want to clear using this process.

Now, let's discuss how the HK Performance Trigger is used to clear the information that surfaced for you during your HK Journaling exercise.

How To Use The HK Performance Trigger

With the onion analogy I explained that the center of the onion represents your capacity to win with more consistency. The layers of synthesizing events that you have accumulated over the years are responsible for preventing you from realizing your true potential.

What's creating problems with your competitive performance right now is the fact that you carry these synthesizing events with you from contest to contest. It's as if you are walking through a mental revolving door. I suggest that you do the HK Journaling the evening after each and every contest in which you compete.

What follows is a four step process that will allow you to peel away the layers of mental blockages responsible for creating the problems you are now experiencing using the coaching scenario:

Step #1: If you haven't already, go back to the chapter on Programming In The HK Performance Trigger. Program in the trigger by following Steps 1 through 3 (Once the trigger is programmed in you never have to do it again);

Step #2: Read your HK Journaling list starting with the negative things that came up for you during your coaching performance and read them one at a time;

Step #3: After reading the first item on the negative side of your list, hit your trigger. Say or mentally state the word "relax" and touch the thumb and index fingers of both hands, and open them. Move to the second negative thing and do the same thing until you have gone through the entire negative list;

Step #4: Now, move to the positive list and repeat Step #3 until you have gone through the entire positive list;

This is extremely effective because your Subconscious Mind stored every aspect of your competitive performance earlier that day. Doing the HK Journaling exercise allows you to access that information from your Subconscious Mind and any mental blockages attached to it

Using the HK Performance Trigger creates a medium whereby you can clear and release those synthesizing events so that you don't carry them with you into your next competition. Here's why this is so effective. Suppose one of the negative things that came up for you during your post competition HK Journaling was that as a coach, you make a bad call during a crucial point in the game that adversely affected the outcome.

When you read that statement, your Conscious Mind will send instructions to your Subconscious Mind, "Send up all the information you have in storage relating to the bad call I made in our game earlier today."

When that information comes up from your Subconscious Mind, it will bring all the mental blockages (synthesizing events) associated with it as well. When you hit your HK Performance Trigger, it allows you to subconsciously clear away yet another layer of this mental onion that has grown around your performance. The HK Performance Trigger will neutralize any synthesizing events that surface during this process.

My suggestion is to punch holes in the completed exercises and keep them in a three ring binder. Once a month or so, review them and see if you can find any patterns that may be developing in your competitive performances that may need addressing.

In fact, the question you should be asking yourself after each contest is, "What could I have done to improve my performance during this contest?" If you don't think this process is effective, Byron Nelson, a former PGA Tour player, won 18 tournaments (11 in a row!) in one year back in the 1940's doing the exact same thing. If it worked for him, it will certainly work for you.

Mind Mastery For Winning

I created a program for competitors called *Mind Mastery For Winning.* It includes the DVD *Change Your Thinking, Change Your Life*, and a powerful 30 minute CD titled *Becoming A Winner.* The DVD explains HK and how I use muscle testing when working with individuals to help them clear blockages preventing them from successfully accomplishing their goals. It will also show you how to muscle test yourself.

The CD is designed and intended to work on a subconscious level and can be used as a pre-game mental preparation regimen that will put you in a mental space that will allow you to perform your best during competition. The same HK Trigger word (relax) is programmed in at the beginning of the CD.

The CD contains over 100 statements relating specifically to winning. Each statement is followed by the trigger word relax. For instance, one of the statements on the CD is, "Release all fear from your mind and body preventing you from becoming a winner." This statement, and all statements on the CD, are followed by the trigger word relax.

Any subconsciously stored fear relating to the statement will surface, and the trigger word "relax" is simply a medium that will allow you to subconsciously neutralize any stress that surfaced relating to the statement. The reason it works is because "Energy Follows Intention!" Repeated listening to the CD will help you peel away layers of synthesizing events from this subconscious onion you have created over the years preventing you from winning more consistenly.

Here is what you do. One to two hours before competition, find a quiet location to sit or recline. Close your eyes and do your best to consciously listen to each statement. Pay close attention to any physiological changes or sensations you may experience in your body after hearing the trigger word "relax." You may find yourself taking a deep breath or yawning. This simply means that a very subtle energy shift is occurring for you on a subconscious level relating to one of the statements you just heard on the CD.

It is recommended that you listen to the CD before and after each competition. If time prevents you from listening to the CD before your competition listen to the CD the night before and the evening after your competition.

The CD is designed to work on a subconscious level because that is where your performance problems are. Listening to the CD before your competition helps you to mentally prepare by clearing out the cobwebs. Listening to the CD after your competition helps to peel away layers of synthesizing events that may have surfaced for you dur ng competition.

Think of your age. That's how old your belief system is. If for instance, you have difficulty winning with any consistency, it is simply your belief system acting out through your physical body. And, it will perpetuate this experience until you take action to change it. Listening to the CD daily allows you to peel away the layers of this onion you have created preventing you from becoming a more consistent winner.

Remember that when stress is present in your body it will also cause one or both hemispheres of your brain to weaken or switch off. It is when the brain is in this weakened state that the sabotaging anomaly will manifest for you.

Listening to the CD coupled with the HK Journaling will provide you with an excellent regimen to help you accelerate the peeling away of the layers of subconsciously stored negative information preventing you from reaching your true potential to win with more consistency.

I cannot stress the important of listening to the CD before and after each game. Even after practice. Sometimes it is difficult for you to take 30 minutes out of your day to sit down and listen to the CD. If this is the case, I suggest that you buy a small portable CD player and place it at the head of you bed. Turn it on before you drift off to sleep with the volume very low and the hit repeat button.

Although the best results will be achieved from listening to the CD while in your waking conscious state, you will still derive substantial benefits from listening to it as you drift off to sleep. Listening to the CD allows you to do everything in your power to become mentally prepared for your upcoming competition. You may also listen to the CD while driving in your car; jogging, etc.

Setting Goals

After Tiger Woods won his first Masters, he skipped a tournament, and came back and won the next tournament. During his post tournament interview, he was asked why he thought he won. Tiger Woods looked at the interviewer surprisingly and replied, "Because it was my goal to win it."

How does your physical body know what your mind expects from it if you do not set a goal? I hate to use cliques, but this one is so appropriate. When you don't set goals, it is like a ship without a rudder. It just spins in circles. ALWAYS SET GOALS!

When you set a goal before your competition one of two things will happen. You will either win or you will have the worst performance you have had in years. Why? Because when you set a goal that is when your "stuff" (synthesizing events) comes up.

I suggest that you set a goal before each competition. Here's what you do. The night before your competition, grab a pencil and paper and write down your goal. After documenting your goal, read it aloud and use your HK Performance Trigger. Let's assume you are a tennis player. Here is how you would set your goal. (This process can be used for any sport)

Example:

Step #1: I, (state your name,) will win my match against (opponent's name), and I will play my best tennis, and I will do my best to make those decisions during the match that supports me in winning. I will remain calm, relaxed and focused on my goal to win the match and I will succeed and I will never do anything to interfere with the success accomplishment of my goal. This or something better;

Step #2: Hit your HK Performance Trigger by stating or thinking the word "relax" and touching the thumb and index fingers of both hands, and opening them;

Step #3: Read your goal aloud again.

You may modify the language to suit your particular sport. Repeating this process before every competition allows your mind an opportunity to communicate your intentions to your physical body that your goal is to win the contest.

Now, if you do not achieve a victory in your match, it simply means that your mental onion needs additional peeling. You still have synthesizing events that need to be cleared. Please do your best to remain objective during this process.

Doing the HK Journaling, setting goals and listening to the CD will help you on the road to accelerating the peeling away of the layers of synthesizing events stopping you from realizing your goal of becoming a more consistent winner during competition.

ALWAYS SET A GOAL TO WIN!

The Hemispheres & Mechanics

It's very important to understand what happens hemispherically to an athlete when they are executing the mechanics of their sport during competition. At some point in their athletic development, every player was shown how to correctly execute the mechanics of their particular sport.

That information was stored somewhere in their Subconscious Mind. What prevents players from accessing that mechanical information during actual competitive situations is stress. Earlier I had mentioned that when there is stress present in an athlete's body that stress causes one or both hemispheres of his brain to weaken or switch off.

This switching off phenomenon affects his thought processes as well as the correct mechanical execution relative to his particular sport. And it affects athletes who compete individually as well as athletes who compete on teams.

When stress is present in an athlete's physical body, it causes his body to weaken. When his body is in this weakened state, he will drop a pass thrown right into his hands in the end zone that may have won the football game, or miss two free throws with one second left that might have won the basketball game.

The presence of stress in the player's physical body is so pervasive that it hampers and dramatically affects both the mental and mechanical functioning of his body. This is the anomaly responsible for adversely altering his play, and will cause him to make uncharacteristic mental or mechanical errors at crucial moments during the game. Here's why.

The right hemisphere of a player's brain controls the left side of his physical body, while the left hemisphere of his brain controls the right side. Let's assume your sport is basketball. When your right hemisphere weakens or switches off during your shot making during a game, it weakens the left side of your physical body.

When you take a shot during a game with a weak left side, it dramatically alters the mechanical dynamics of that particular shot and will more than likely cause you to miss. There is no way you can consistently play your best with your body in this weakened state. This weakened state is so subtle it cannot be seen with the naked eye, and that is where muscle testing comes in.

This switching off phenomenon not only affects you physically, but mentally as well. For instance, if a basketball player is in his left hemisphere when playing a game, he will have a tendency to play conservatively and may pass the ball rather than take an open shot. Conversely, if the player is in his right hemisphere he will take a low percentage shot rather than pass to an open man. You can see how this phenomenon can adversely affect a player's mental continuity during competition.

Using your HK Trigger during competition will help you keep both hemispheres of your brain switched on so that both sides of your body remain strong allowing you to consistently execute your physical movements resulting in more continuity in your shot making and overall athletic performance.

Using Your Imagination During Practice

Imagination is defined as, "The action or faculty of forming mental images or concepts of what is not actually present to the senses." When you imagine yourself doing something, you are going to subconsciously access the same information as if you were physically doing it. Using imagination during practice is extremely effective because it has a twofold benefit.

First, since imagination is located in the right hemisphere of your brain, every time you use it you are exercising that part of your brain. If you can keep the right hemisphere of your brain switched on during your practice sessions, you will keep it switched on during the actual game.

Secondly, your Subconscious Mind cannot distinguish between something real or imagined. If you don't believe me try telling someone who has a fear of heights that they have nothing to be afraid of. You will fail miserably. That's because the thought of going near a high place creates so much stress in the individual's body that they do not even want to go there mentally.

To get the most out of your practice use your imagination to simulate stressful game situation and see if you can make the shot. If you miss the shot ask yourself, "Why did I miss that shot to win the game?" and hit your trigger. Then attempt the same shot using the same scenario. Here is why this is so effective.

When you ask the question, "Why did I miss that shot to win the game?" your Conscious

Mind will send instructions to your Subconscious Mind, "Send me all the information you have stored relating to why I missed this shot to win the game." If any synthesizing events are accessed during this process, your HK Performance Trigger will neutralize them. This process can be done with any competitive sport.

Imagination is so effective that during the final round of the 1994 United States Women's Open Golf Championships, Lauri Merten was on the practice putting green imagining herself putting to win the tournament. Four hours later she was hoisting the trophy as the 1994 United States Women's Golf Open champion. Imagination is a very powerful and effective tool, and it works. I entreat you to integrate imagination into your practice regime.

Winning

Before you can understand what it takes to become a winner it is important to look at the etymology of the word win. The word win comes from the Greek word "winnen" which literally means "to struggle or contend." However, when we look at Webster's definition of win, we get a different meaning.

Webster's defines win as, "to gain a victory; be victorious; triumph; to finish in first place in a race, contest, etc." What makes a winner? Well, there must be information stored in his belief system to support him in winning. Webster's defines belief as, "something believed; opinion; conviction; confidence in the truth or existence of something not immediately susceptible to rigorous proof."

What kinds of beliefs, opinions, or convictions do you have about yourself relating to winning? What form of rigorous proof can you give me that you are a winner? In order to create a winning belief system, you must first become aware of the information you have stored in your belief system relating to winning. Self-awareness is crucial to effecting positive change. You cannot change something you are not aware of.

If your thoughts create your experiences, you must first change your thoughts relating to winning. Once this happens, your experience will change. The intention of this program is to help you remove the synthesizing events preventing you from winning with more consistency.

Conclusion

I know it is a hard pill for some people to swallow, but it is absolutely imperative that you accept responsibility for the experiences you create both during competition and in your personal life. I don't suggest it so that you can beat yourself up for all the turmoil in your life.

I suggest it so you can get to the second stage of the change process which is, "If I am creating this experience what can I do to change it?" A funny thing happens when you asked yourself this question. Things start to change.

It is said that "Adversity introduces a man to himself." It is my wish that when you encounter adversity during the course of your competitive experiences, that you will not only know where it came from, but be able to conquer it effectively using HK and the disciplines outlined in this book.

I don't specifically know what you are going to have to do to become a winner, but on some level of your awareness you do. Using this program faithfully will help you peel away the synthesizing events preventing you from accessing that information so that you can realize your goal of becoming a more consistent winner no matter what the sport or competition.

To gain the maximum benefit from this program it is important to use the entire program, which entails:

- Programming in the HK Trigger;
- Faithfully using HK Journaling after each competition by documenting negative and positive information relating to your performance;
- Listening to the CD "Becoming A Winner" before and after each competition.
- Always set a goal to win!

In closing, please remember that we are dealing with a tremendous amount of information in your subconscious mind relating to winning that has been stored over a period of many years. Please do your best to remain objective while using this program.

I trust that I have given you a perspective that will allow you to more fully understand how your Mind influences your performance during competition. And, that I have provided you with a remedy that will accelerate positive changes for you that will help you achieve peak performance, not only during your competitive experiences, but ultimately improve the quality of your personal life as well.

A wise man wrote years ago that we can't be Batman to all the Robins in the world. You cannot control what other people think of your, but you can control what you think of you.

Please remember that competition, like life is relative, and that among the blind, the one eyed man is King. "Relax."

***

HK Mind Mastery programs:

Mastery For Golf
Mind Mastery For Soccer
Mind Mastery For Tennis
Mind Mastery For Hitting
Mind Mastery For Pitching
Mind Mastery For Coaching
Mind Mastery For Basketball
Mind Mastery For Winning
Mind Mastery For Learning
Mind Mastery For Money
Mind Mastery For Selling
Mind Mastery For Weight Loss
Mind Mastery For Peace of Mind
Change Your Thinking Change Your Life (DVD)

Other books by Ernest Solivan:

Quantum Psychophysics (A Treatise on HK)
Mastering The Mental Side of Soccer
Mastering The Mental Side of Tennis
Mastering The Mental Side of Hitting
Mastering The Mental Side of Football
Mastering The Mental Side of Pitching
Mastering The Mental Side of Coaching
Mastering The Mental Side of Basketball
Mastering The Mental Side of Putting
Mastering The Mental Side of Tournament Golf
Pro Se Cites & Authorities

For more information about HK contact:
Performance Consultants International
Website: www.hk-relax.com
(All products also available at Amazon.com)

www.ingramcontent.com/pod-product-compliance
Lightning Source LLC
Chambersburg PA
CBHW021343090426
42742CB00008B/718